TABLE OF CONTENTS

FOREWORD 7

ACKNOWLEDGEMENTS 9

ENDORSEMENTS 11

INTRODUCTION 15

WHAT IS ETIQUETTE? 17

RULES OF SOCIAL ETIQUETTE 19

RULES OF DINNER ETIQUETTE 63

RULES OF CHURCH ETIQUETTE 79

RULES OF TELEPHONE ETIQUETTE 91

ABOUT THE AUTHOR 103

Things My Mother "Never" Told Me About Etiquette

Lady Lisa Hicks

Things My Mother "NEVER" Told Me About Etiquette

Things My Mother "Never" Told Me About Etiquette
Copyright © 2016 by Lady Lisa Hicks

All rights reserved. No part of this book may be reproduced or transmitted in any form or by any means without written permission from the author.

ISBN 9781530367184
Printed in USA

Things My Mother "NEVER" Told Me About Etiquette

Foreword

It has been my privilege to know Lady Lisa Hicks for 22 years. The words that describe her are not mere words of formality or flattery. That would be an insult to this Christian woman. **Humble** describes her. She has been honored by many a church, group, and organization. However, whenever I see her, she genuinely hugs me, making me certain that she is glad to see me. **Gracious** further describes her as she uninhibitedly shares with others publically and without reservation. **Graceful** is another of her characteristics. She understands her place in God's Kingdom and serves Him and His people with love and kindness. She is ***dynamic***, as well. When she stands before the people of God to deliver His word, the power of the Spirit strengthens her as she unashamedly ministers. I have often thought, *"You have to hold onto your hat when Missionary Lisa ministers."*

I had the opportunity to be in her workshop after she wrote and published her first book, ***Things My Mother Never Told Me About Marriage.*** It was there that I realized she had the correct concept of marriage, according to the Scriptures, and that she was all too willing to pass it on to others who needed her guidance. So, it is really no surprise that her new book, ***Things My Mother Never Told Me About Etiquette*** is a necessary book that will further edify the saints. She is humorous and energetic in her delivery of everyday common behaviors that many don't even know about. ***Things My Mother Never Told Me About Etiquette*** will let readers know that God is interested in all areas of His children's lives.

There are other words I can use to describe her, but suffice it to say that she is one of God's best. A wife, mother and grandmother, Lady Lisa exemplifies the kind of virtuous, Christian woman needed in this 21st Century. She is a woman "…for such a time as this."

Rosa Worth, friend and Editor
It's Worth Editing & Administrative Services

Things My Mother "NEVER" Told Me About Etiquette

Acknowledgements

With my heart full of loving emotions I would like to acknowledge the many people who saw me through this book by expressing my gratitude to all those who provided support, talked things over, read, offered comments, allowed me to quote some of their remarks and assisted in the editing, proofreading and design of **Things My Mother "Never" Told Me About Etiquette**

More specifically, I would like to thank: Holly Harrison, my sister for all of her constant words of encouragement. Whenever, I would let the book writing process die down, she would always lend her supportive words by consistently reminding me to continue my book project without stopping until it was completed.

In addition to my sister, I have to acknowledge my wonderful daughters; Krystal and Angel, for our many brainstorming sessions when making this book come to life. They were always willing and ready to lend a listening ear during my countless phone calls concerning book ideas and thoughts. You two are THE BEST!

Last but not least, above all I have to acknowledge my awesome husband; Pastor Zachary N. Hicks for allowing me the time to focus on getting the book done. Although, the process was time consuming at times; I appreciate the "Go Ahead" I receive from him when the Lord lays something on my heart to do. I love you!

Things My Mother "NEVER" Told Me About Etiquette

Endorsements

After reading Lady Lisa's first book, ***Things My Mother Never Told Me about Marriage***, I knew her follow-up book; ***Things My Mother Never Told Me About Etiquette*** would be an excellent choice to read. As a Pastor of a church I often find myself reading many different books regardless of the topic; in an effort to expand my knowledge to help others. I have found Lady Lisa's books to be excellent resources for personal self-help as well as for teaching and training sessions. Just as in her previous book, The rules in this etiquette book are also short, simple, humorous, and straight to the point. They are all extremely useful and will help enhance many areas of people's lives.

Pastor Barry Kelso
Faith Clinic Ministries
Barnesville, GA

Things My Mother "Neve"r Told Me about Etiquette is a good book. Lady Lisa gives her thoughts on being a proper woman in today's society. I decided to read the book to get a better understanding of these etiquette rules, because as a father, I want to raise proper young ladies. Therefore, when I heard the title of the book I was instantly intrigued. I wanted to read the book for myself before purchasing a few for my daughters. Needless to say, the things I read in the book were wonderful tips and guidelines for being a lady with class and excellent etiquette.

Johnny E Bentley III, Manager
Bentley & Sons Funeral Home
Thomaston, GA

As an etiquette coach for many young girls and being responsible for teaching them the proper way to act as 'little ladies with class and poise', I often find myself reading the latest books on etiquette. ***Things My Mother Never Told Me about Etiquette*** was a great choice to read for information to utilize when trying to teach young girls how to be women with class. The way in which the information is presented in the book allows me to use the book as a teacher's manual for my class. The rules are simply put, easy to comprehend, and there is more than enough information given in the rules to allow me to provide additional information for my students.

Miss Joyce Jacobs
Etiquette Coach

Things My Mother "NEVER" Told Me About Etiquette

As a male fashion designer, personal shopper, and stylist for men, and a majority of women in high profile positions; I have to be professional, courteous, and very polite. In other words I have to show and prove etiquette in every interaction with my clients. Therefore, when I learned one of my very own clients, Lady Lisa Hicks, authored an etiquette book; I had to read it. Not only does Lady Lisa engulf and demonstrate the rules in her book but she is also extremely down to earth, friendly, and just plain nice in real life. She also did a good job showing her own characteristics within the pages of her book. It is a very easy read that is not only enjoyable but also very helpful. If you are thinking about getting it, think no longer…It is a MUST read.

J. Rantzler
Stylist

A woman of God, a woman of class, and a woman with a great deal of wisdom to communicate to the women of God. As a Superintendent for a school district in Pontiac, MI, I am constantly attacked by the enemy to adhere to my flesh and respond in a way that is not of God. However, Missionary Lisa has proven over and over again (leading by example) that a woman of *class* is revered. I have studied this woman for years and I am amazed at the Godly traits that she not only possesses, but also teaches to others. Missionary Lisa teaches where no other woman of God dares to go. She teaches about etiquette and how a woman should represent herself not just publicly, but privately, as well. If you are not amazed and don't take heed to the advice given in this book (and her previous books), then you are not ready to advance to the next level of your life, your God given purpose.

Septembra Williams, M.Ed.
Superintendent/CAO
Arts & Technology Academy of Pontiac

Things My Mother "Neve"r Told Me about Etiquette is a must read! It is an invaluable book of wisdom, providing helpful advice and tools for women of all ages on how to be a woman of elegance.

Pamela J. Moore
Detroit Medical Center
Director AR Management I

I have been privileged to work with Lady Lisa for approximately 23 years. I have a lot of respect for her work and dedication to educate others in many areas of life. Lady Lisa has garnered a lot of knowledge and experience over the years in how to behave properly in many environments, which is why I highly recommend this book for men and women. You will learn how to use proper etiquette while in the company of others. You will learn how to act and not act in public places; as well as when to speak and not speak. Great advice and teaching by Lady Lisa Hicks.

Mrs. Earletta Bailey
Executive Administrative Assistant
Faith Clinic Church of God in Christ
Detroit, MI

It is not only an honor but an absolute pleasure to endorse this marvelous book authored by Lady Lisa Hicks. The book, **Things My Mother Never Told Me about Etiquette** gives etiquette rules to be mindful of when interacting with people in almost every aspect of life. This book is not your typical book on "etiquette". It does not stick to advice pertaining to the same ordinary etiquette training such as: Dining Etiquette, Professional Etiquette, or Social Etiquette. Lady Lisa gives A to Z etiquette advice in a humorous non-offensive tone. The etiquette rules in this book range from simple common sense etiquette, such as: "Say Please and Thank You", to etiquette rules that are probably thought but never spoken out loud such as: "Never Air your Dirty Laundry on Social Media for everyone to see, Keep it in your home and wash it there". Needless to say, this book is an absolute must read! You will not be disappointed!!!

Mrs. Krystal Lovejoy, M.Ed.
Certified Family Life Educator
Detroit, MI

I highly recommend this book!!! If you have young ladies in your life, they need this book as a guide. With all of the events and special occasions that we as women may engage in on a daily basis, this book will show you how and when to use good proper manners. From taking and receiving compliments to knowing when to talk and when to listen, how to tip, and having good table manners. Lady Lisa pretty much addresses it all. Several great rules for your everyday lady.

Laketa Edmon
State of Michigan
Disability Examiner Assistant

Introduction

In today's society, women are expected to know how to act and to show etiquette in every situation and arena of life. These proper behaviors are typically learned from your mother while growing up as a young girl. However, *my* personal knowledge was learned through mistakes made with or without correction. In addition to the mistakes, I found myself observing the behaviors of others during my daily life and living.

Things My Mother "Never" Told Me about Etiquette is a combination of my many years of trial and error. As a young lady growing up in the South and not having much money, I did not go to many functions that required etiquette or table manners; especially since we were barely eating. However, as I grew up and began dealing with people and going to formal affairs, I realized the need for proper etiquette. Some things I learned the hard way and some I learned by studying. So, while some of these rules are short, humorous and just plain common sense they are also designed to instruct and encourage you to have good or better etiquette. Within this easy reading book you will find the rules range from social etiquette, to dinner etiquette, to church etiquette, all the way to simple phone etiquette.

But Wait! Don't worry because the meaning for each set of etiquette rules is clearly explained to ensure that ***men and women*** understand the differences and reasons for each specific set of rules. So, come along as we confront the everyday situations that beg us for a proper etiquette response.

Things My Mother "NEVER" Told Me About Etiquette

What is Etiquette?

Etiquette is basically the customary code of gracious and polite behavior in society or among members of a particular profession or group.

Things My Mother "NEVER" Told Me About Etiquette

Rules of Social Etiquette

Social Etiquette is formal manners and rules that are followed in social or professional settings.

Things My Mother "NEVER" Told Me About Etiquette

Rule #1

'Say Hello'

Say "Hello" upon entrance! When you enter into a room, it is proper to speak. In fact, you shouldn't wait for someone to speak to you, but upon your entrance you should say hello and smile.

"A man that hath friends must shew himself friendly..."

~Proverbs 11:24a

Rule #2

'Help Clean Up'

Can I Help? You've been invited to dinner at a friend's house. The respectable thing to do is to offer assistance with cleaning up. A simple, "Can I help?" means a lot to someone who has prepared and served dinner for guests at his or her home.

"Use hospitality one to another…"

~I Peter 4:9

Rule #3

'Be On Time'

Be RESPECTFUL of other people's time! When you schedule a meeting, make sure you are not the LAST one walking in. BE ON TIME!!!! In fact, when scheduling a meeting, add a minimum of thirty minutes lead time to ensure that you, the organizer are on time.

Being late is thought to be disrespectful, especially when *you* scheduled the meeting. In the event that being late is unavoidable, COMMUNICATE! COMMUNICATE with the other party in a timely manner.

Things My Mother "NEVER" Told Me About Etiquette

Rule #4

'Excuse Yourself

Excuse me! Have you ever walked in a store and needed to pass someone? A simple 'Excuse me' will lessen the opportunity for the other person to feel threatened.

Rule #5

'Thank You'

It's only right that if someone does something for you say, 'Thank You.' Showing appreciation to someone for being nice is a wonderful way to say thank you. But, how do you say thank you besides verbally? Send a note of appreciation; send an email, a nice text message, purchase a greeting card etc. A simple 'Thank You' goes a long way.

Rule #6

'You-Not Your Friends'

You alone were invited! When someone invites you to a function, it's good practice to ask before you include others in the invitation. PLEASE! PLEASE! PLEASE! DO NOT show up with your friends as a +3 to an event without asking. In fact, if the invitation was directed to you, especially at someone's home, it is poor etiquette to bring extra people.

Rule #7

'Be Quiet'

Keep All Eyes Off You! Refrain from being loud in public places that cause others to draw their attention to you. Your conversation should never exceed the ears of those closest to you and even they may not want to hear your conversation.

Things My Mother "NEVER" Told Me About Etiquette

Rule #8

'Respect Your Elders'

Acknowledge those who are older than you! It's unbelievable that this needs to be stated, but there remains a need for this reminder. Be courteous to older people; hold the door for them; and provide them a seat when seating is limited.

"Stand up in the presence of the aged, show respect for the elderly and revere your God. I am the LORD."

~Leviticus 19:32

Rule #9

'Acknowledge'

Who's your friend? If you are talking to someone and another person approaches, acknowledge and introduce the new person.

Rule #10

'P!P!P!'

Posture, Position & Poise! Don't slouch! Sit Up Straight! Your posture says a lot about you and your position speaks before you ever open your mouth.

Rule #11

'Show Some Teeth'

The value of a smile! Learn to smile because it creates a welcoming environment. Compliment others with a smile or other verbal communication.

Things My Mother "NEVER" Told Me About Etiquette

Rule #12

'Quit Being Nosey'

Don't just make yourself at home! Be respectful when visiting someone's home. Walking around the house without permission is disrespectful. Wait until you are invited to tour the house. Ask permission before you go around the house. Do not look into people's cabinets and closets.

"And that ye study to be quiet, and to do your own business…"
I Thessalonians 4:11

Rule #13

'Self-Control'

Maintain self-control! Learn and practice how to keep your attitude under control, even in the most out of control situations. Refrain from lashing out by controlling your emotions.

Rule #14

'Shut-Up'

The same letters used to spell listen, also spell silent! Refrain from cutting a person off when in conversation. Listen attentively to what they are saying before interjecting. Effective communication allows both parties to speak and to be heard.

Rule #15

'Watch that Coughing and Sneezing'

It is next to impossible not to cough or sneeze, especially if there are irritants present (dust, perfume, cologne, etc.) or some personal discomfort. However, it is a must that when you have to sneeze or cough that you cover your mouth using a napkin or tissue or the bend of your arm. Never sneeze or cough into your hands, as that passes germs.

Rule #16

'Eye Contact'

Can you see me? In some cultures it is impolite and dishonorable to refuse eye contact. Be sure to make eye contact with the person you are in communication with. Avoid the uncomfortable staring into one's eyes, unless of course it's your significant other; but by all means make eye contact.

Rule #17

'Don't be a Garbage Can'

If they'll do it with you, they'll do it to you! Refuse to gossip with or about your friends. When someone brings you gossip, refuse to hear it and leave the location if you must. Don't forget a dog that will bring a bone will carry a bone!

Rule #18

'Don't be a Bum'

Bring something to the table! When you are invited to a party or function, especially in someone's home, bring something to share: A nice dessert, beverage (appropriately chosen) or even a dish. If you are uncertain, you can always ask, "Can I bring something?"

Rule #19

'Know When to Leave'

Don't overstay your welcome! When you are invited to someone's home, subconsciously plan to stay no longer than an hour past the festivities; unless you are invited to stay longer. Please! Please! Please! Don't wait until the host has on his or her night clothes before you get the hint to leave.

Rule #20

'Pay Back'

Borrowing implies that you will be paying it back! If you borrow money from someone, be sure to pay it back according to the terms agreed upon. If you cannot pay back the money, say that up front. You don't want to be on Judge Judy.

Rule #21

'Can You Read?'

Read the event to be sure! Some invites are "Adults Only" and it would be a shame to bring your child without permission. If the invite specifies and you haven't asked, you might need to stay home with your child or risk being sent home with your child. If that happens do not get offended.

Things My Mother "NEVER" Told Me About Etiquette

Rule #22

'A Car Don't Run on Air'

Everyone is on a budget! When someone agrees to provide you with transportation to and from a destination, it's only right to offer them gas money. No, you don't have to fill up the tank, but the offer alone is a sign of appreciation.

Rule #23

'Stop It!'

Do not air your dirty laundry on social media! Please put it in the washing machine in the privacy of your own home. Not everything belongs on social media!

Things My Mother "NEVER" Told Me About Etiquette

Rule #24

'RSVP'

When you are invited to a function and an RSVP is requested, don't wait until the last minute to do it. That shows a lack of consideration for the host who is planning the event. Timeliness with your RSVP is just as important as you being an invited guest.

Rule #25

'No Show'

Please do not RSVP for an event or function, and then do not show up. That is considered RUDE! It can also cost your host unnecessary expense because of your lack of etiquette.

Rule #26

'Decline'

If you can't attend an event that you're formally invited to, please do not assume that not RSVP'ing is the same as declining. If you cannot make it to the event, respectfully decline by the indicated RSVP date.

Rule #27

'Yuck! Wash Your Hands'

Please! Please! Please! Wash your hands after going to the restroom. It's quite simple to do. Once you finish using the restroom, go over to the sink and use the soap and water to wash your hands. Don't forget to use a napkin to open the restroom door when leaving; not doing so could expose you to more germs.

Rule #28

'Let Me Rest'

If you go the hospital to visit someone ill, keep your visit short. Please do not stay for an hour or longer. Remember, a patient in the hospital NEEDS rest.

Rule #29

'Too Much Information'

When visiting an ill person do not tell them about someone you know that has passed away from his or her same illness. You should have stayed home with that type of inconsiderate information!

Rule #30

'Buy Some Gas'

If you borrow someone's car please don't return the car with the gas tank on "E" and the outside dirty. Show some appreciation and replace at minimum the gas you used. Also, if you picked up the car looking like a shiny new dime, do not return it looking like a rusty penny. Otherwise, you will more than likely never use the car again.

Rule #31

'Break Wind'

It is impolite to "break wind" in the presence of another person. In the event you cannot hold it in, please excuse yourself!

Things My Mother "NEVER" Told Me About Etiquette

Rule #32

'Mints, Please'

Don't offend with your breath when you know you will be talking close to someone's face. Keep some mints with you. If speaking without mints is unavoidable and you know your breath is not welcoming, please speak from a courteous distance!

Rule #33

'Only a Mistake'

If you bump someone by mistake, be courteous and say, "EXCUSE ME." While we all make mistakes, it's important to remember that a simple 'Excuse Me' can disarm a volatile situation and protect you and others from harm.

Rule #34

'Train Up A Child'

Not the right place! Refrain from allowing your children to act unseemly or carry on as they would at a gym when visiting a restaurant. You have seen the child who is crawling under the table, throwing things, and touching people. A restaurant is NOT Chuck E. Cheeses (where a KID really *can* be a KID)

Rule #35

'Get Permission'

It is rude to take pictures or videos at an event and post them on social media without the host's permission. Please do not make people feel they need to attach a 'no photographs or no video recording' disclosure to your invite. It is a good and accepted rule not to post pictures of events until the host has done so or clear permission has been given.

Things My Mother "NEVER" Told Me About Etiquette

Rule #36

'Proper Appearance'

Please take time to make sure your appearance is nice and polished. It is good practice to ensure you look neat and clean whenever you leave your house. The first thing a person notices is the way you look. A nice appearance shows you value yourself and what other people think of you.

Rule #37

'Proper Clothing'

Please refrain from wearing clothing that is inappropriate for the occasion. When attending a specific function, be certain you are dressed for the occasion. Do not wear a *Party Dress* to a *Business Meeting* and do not put on your best *Church Suit* for a *Saturday Picnic*.

Things My Mother "NEVER" Told Me About Etiquette

Rule #38

'Don't be a Blabber Mouth'

Respecting other people means that you respect their wishes. If someone tells you a secret in confidence, please respect their wishes and keep it confidential. If you are a blabber mouth and you can't help but tell everything you hear, then be upfront and honest and inform the other person, "I am a Blabber Mouth and I will more than likely tell your secret!" This will allow your friend to make an informed decision to tell you the secret or NOT.

Rule #39

'Don't Be Rude'

Please refrain from being rude when someone is speaking to you. It is improper etiquette to sigh, roll your eyes or look into space with a blank stare when someone is talking to you. Your body language is a clear indication of being interested in or not interested in what a person is saying. If you are disinterested in what someone is saying, be respectful and at least smile and nod so you won't appear rude.

Things My Mother "NEVER" Told Me About Etiquette

Rule #40

'Throw Your Gum into the Trash'

Please refrain from sticking your chewing gum under the chair, table or any other place that is not the trash. If you are chewing gum and no longer want it, please remove it from your mouth with a napkin or piece of paper (if napkins are not available) and throw it away.

Rule #41

'Shower! Shower! Shower!'

Please refrain from going around others when you have not showered properly. A body odor is considered offensive. A person should always smell pleasant in public or in the presence of other people. If you do not care to use a perfume or cologne, soap and water will suffice.

Things My Mother "NEVER" Told Me About Etiquette

Rules of Dinner Etiquette

Dinner Etiquette is the set of manners and behaviors that are expected of a person while eating.

Rule #42

'Refrain from Electronics'

Dinner is a time to be social with those in front of you, not those on SOCIAL MEDIA. Refrain from using any of the multiple electronic devices (cell phone, I Pad, I Pod, tablet, etc.) available to get on to social media while you are at dinner. In fact, place the electronic device face down on the table or in your pocket or purse to refrain from use during dinner.

Rule #43

'Nose No-No!'

Please don't blow your nose at the table. You may be sick, but now you are making others sick—people are eating. Excuse yourself from the table and go to a secluded space (preferably the restroom) and blow your nose.

Things My Mother "NEVER" Told Me About Etiquette

Rule #44

'Don't Take Advantage'

Please, no carry outs! When you are invited to a dinner function, it's impolite to take a carryout without the permission of the host. Even more, it's totally disrespectful to pack a carryout before all the guests have eaten. If given permission, remember less is better. Don't try to pack a weeks' worth of food; a small doggie bag is acceptable.

Things My Mother "NEVER" Told Me About Etiquette

Rule #45

'Close Your Mouth'

Never eat and talk with your mouth full of food. That is gross! Yes, it can be hard to carry on a conversation at the dinner table, but it isn't impossible. In the event that you are asked a question while you are eating, pause and give the hand gesture that you need a moment. Once you've finished eating the food, place your fork on the plate, and then finish with the conversation. Everyone at the table will appreciate it; but most importantly, you won't have food falling out of your mouth.

Things My Mother "NEVER" Told Me About Etiquette

Rule #46

'No Touching'

Refrain from hand shaking when eating! Instead use verbal communication to acknowledge someone's presence and refrain from touching.

Rule #47

'Can You Wait'

Restaurant service can be unreliable and untimely, but you can help make everyone's dining experience enjoyable. Don't eat before everyone's food has arrived at the table, unless you have a medical condition, and then at least acknowledge it to others before doing so.

Things My Mother "NEVER" Told Me About Etiquette

Rule #48

'Face Down'

Your phone has no place at the table during a formal dinner. However, if you cannot leave it in your pocket, place your phone on silent and in the face down position at a formal dinner. Unless totally unavoidable, leave the room to take a call or send a text message.

Rule #49

'Watch Your Reach'

Please pass the dish! Reaching over the table for a roll is not proper etiquette. The favorable thing to do is to ask someone to pass you the item nearest them. Only reach for those items within arm's reach of your seat and that doesn't invade the space of other dinner guests.

Things My Mother "NEVER" Told Me About Etiquette

Rule #50

'Napkin? A Must'

The napkin was created for you! Use your napkin to wipe your mouth and hands at the table and refrain from using your hands and fingers. Sometimes dinner can get messy, but your napkin is your savior. Hands dirty? Clean them up with a napkin.

Things My Mother "NEVER" Told Me About Etiquette

Rule #51

'Pay Your Way'

Gratuity is a must! When you are out to dinner with a large group, always be prepared to pay for your meal and leave a tip. Taking for granted that someone will cover your meal is disrespectful and might leave you uninvited in the future.

Things My Mother "NEVER" Told Me About Etiquette

Rule #52

'Outside-IN'

When at a dinner with place settings, it can become difficult to remember which utensil to utilize at which time during the course of dinner. Please remember to start with the utensils on the outside and work your way to inside utensils.

Rule #53

'Your Napkin'

When sitting down at dinner, please remember to place your napkin over your lap as soon as you are seated. This will help prevent staining your clothes if something falls or spills onto your lap while at dinner.

Rule #54

'Chew Your Food'

Please take your time to chew your food when eating at a dinner table. Do not just bite your food and just swallow. You are NOT a turkey, *Do Not Gobble* down your food.

Rule #55

'Finger Licking Good!'

Please refrain from licking your fingers while at dinner. Yes, the food may be finger licking good, but that is not literal. Your fingers are NOT food. If your hands are sticky from the food you are eating, please ask the waitress for a wet napkin.

Lady Lisa Hicks

Rule #56

'Proper Conversation'

While at dinner, please refrain from discussing gross things or talking about subjects that are not considered proper etiquette for a dinner table. Choose your conversation wisely while eating; otherwise you can possibly make someone sick during dinner! Remember dinner is for good times and good fellowship.

Rules of Church Etiquette

Church Etiquette is a set of rules that govern behavior in the House of God.

Rule #57

'Put the Food Away'

Please do not EAT in the sanctuary! ALL eating and drinking is to be done in the Fellowship Hall Area. Eating is ALWAYS prohibited in the sanctuary!

Rule #58

'No Parading'

Punctuality! Be on time for church. If being late is unavoidable for any reason, please sit in the back and don't parade down the aisle; unless other instructions are given by the usher.

Rule #59

'Button Your Lip'

Please, NO talking during Church! This is a time to communicate with God and not your friends. Besides being disrespectful to God, it is rude to others in the church who are trying to worship. If it is an absolute must for you to talk to someone, then get to church early and have your "meeting" beforehand. You can always wait until church is dismissed and talk in the Fellowship Hall afterwards.

Rule #60

'Wake-Up'

Don't sleep in church during service! Sleeping during service is rude to the Pastor or Speaker. If it seems impossible to stay awake try siting up straight, take some notes, or pop a mint in your mouth. The church pew is not your bed!

Rule #61

'Vibrate'

Please don't use your cell phone to talk or text in church during service! PUT IT AWAY!! If you have a situation that requires you to keep your cell phone on, turn it on silent or vibrate and answer it outside the sanctuary if needed.

Rule #62

'Stop Walking'

Don't walk at inappropriate times during service! Please do not walk when individuals are reading the scriptures or during prayer. If you are walking and someone begins to read the scripture or begins to pray, STOP and stand still until they are finish.

Rule #63

'The Communion Table'

The Communion Table is "sacred" and should be used for the Holy Ordinance of the Church ONLY. Please don't put personal items on the communion table. Also, it is not to be used as another table in the fellowship hall.

Rule #64

'No Reserved Seating'

Please refrain from reserving seats in church. Allow others to sit as they come into the church, and especially make room for visitors—slide down so they can feel welcome. Church is not a restaurant; it does not have Reserved Seating unless specified by the leadership.

"Let us consider one another to provoke unto love and to good works"

~Hebrews 10:24

Rule #65

'Watch Your Mouth'

We must use language in the church that honors God! Please NO swearing in the House of the Lord. This is not the Devil's House!

"Let no corrupt communication proceed out of your mouth, but that which is good to the use of edifying, that it may minister grace unto the hearers."

~Ephesians 4:29

Rule #66

'The Pulpit'

The pulpit is a sacred area! Please don't use it as a hangout spot. It should be used for the clergy and any speakers invited into the pulpit. We must train our children that this is a sacred area in the sanctuary and not a play area.

Rules of Telephone Etiquette

Telephone Etiquette refers to a set of rules that apply when people make calls to others or when they are receiving phone calls.

Things My Mother "NEVER" Told Me About Etiquette

Rule #67

'Speaker Phone'

If you take a call on speaker phone, please let your caller know immediately. Everyone should not hear your conversation. It is okay to answer a call and put it on speaker phone while you are driving. However, it is your responsibility to let the other person know that you have them on speaker phone. When you receive a call you can answer by saying, "Hello, you are on speaker." This allows the caller to make an adjustment to their statement, but most importantly acknowledge if he or she should be taken off speaker phone.

Rule #68

'Three-Way'

Please don't put a person on a 3-way phone conversation without his or her knowledge of it. If you do call someone with another person already on the phone; inform the new caller immediately or ask permission of the new person before even connecting the calls. Please don't be sneaky!

Rule #69

'Short and Sweet'

Consider the length of your phone calls! Have you ever had someone who talked so long, that you filter all their future calls through your voicemail? Short and sweet conversations work better than long and drawn out communications. When making calls, be ready, be quick, and be thankful!

Rule #70

'Consider My Ears'

Consider my ears! We've all taken a call while at dinner or maybe in a car with loud music, but it don't make it right. Before you take that call, consider the ears of the person on the other end. No one wants to hear chewing or loud music while trying to complete a call. If the noise is unavoidable, acknowledge it to the other party as a courtesy.

Rule #71

'Appropriate Conversations'

Please avoid discussing things in public that are considered personal or confidential while on the cell phone. If you must talk in public about something personal or confidential go into an area away from others to speak privately so no one else can hear your conversation. There is a thing known as people that Ear Hustle!

Rule #72

'Don't Abuse Call Waiting'

If you are on the phone and another caller clicks in, please do not leave the initial caller waiting on hold forever. When you have a caller on hold and the second conversation will not be brief; be considerate and let the first caller know you will call him or her back.

Rule #73

'Finish Your Food First'

Please refrain from answering the phone or calling someone while you are eating. It is improper etiquette to chew food and smack in someone's ear while on the phone. You can at least finish eating first before making a call or answering a call or else you will have someone asking what you are having for lunch.

Rule #74

'One at a Time!'

Please refrain from carrying on simultaneous conversations while on the phone. Do not talk to someone in your background while talking on your cell phone to someone else. If you are talking to someone in the same room as you, please finish that conversation before making a call. If someone calls your phone, ask the person in your background to hold on while you finish your phone conversation.

Rule #75

'Be Courteous and Return Calls'

Please do not be inconsiderate by not returning your calls. It is only common sense to return a missed call in a timely manner. Ideally, a 24-hour turn around for a return call is proper etiquette. If a voicemail is left specifying the best return call time and date then try to be respectful of the message.

About the Author

Lady Lisa Hicks,

Is very humble and has a deep and abiding love for the Lord and for people. According to Lady Hicks, one of her purposes in life is to work with women of all ages, as well as to encourage them to become all they have been ordained to be.

Superintendent Zachary Hicks and Lady Lisa Hicks have been married for over thirty seven years and have four children and ten grandchildren. Lady Hicks has been instrumental in the growth of the ministry. Lady Hicks is known for her messages of inspiration, hope and encouragement. She is a much sought after workshop teacher, conference speaker and revivalist. She is a Marriage Coach to women for over 23 years. She is a speaker for Married Couples Conferences and Retreats along with her husband. She is also known for her dynamic workshop entitled the "Proverbs 31 Woman".

Every Tuesday, they are partners with Forgotten Harvest in providing food to approximately 300 families in the community. Her dream is to build her own One-Stop Facility for homeless and battered women with children called "LADY LISA'S HOUSE". Having founded many of the ministries, she continues to work tirelessly in all that her hands find to do to include the following:

- Founder, Will Thou Be Made Whole Women's Ministry (For women that have been abused, wounded, have become broken and fragmented in their lives.)
- Co-Founder of Love N Kindness Veterans Housing
- Co-Founder of Love Outreach Service Center (Rehabilitation/Shelter for Men with children)
- Vice President of Edgar & Easter Hicks Bible Institute/Destiny School of Ministry
- Co-Founder of Faith Clinic Ministries in Barnesville, Georgia and Faith Clinic Christian Center in Thomaston, GA
- Author of "Things My Mother 'Never' Me About Marriage"
- Serves under the leadership of 1st Assistant Presiding Bishop P.A. Brooks and Mother Norma Burrell in the Northeast Michigan Jurisdiction Church of God in Christ.

Things My Mother "NEVER" Told Me About Etiquette